Early Church Classics.

ST. CYPRIAN
ON
THE LORD'S PRAYER

*AN ENGLISH TRANSLATION, WITH
INTRODUCTION*

BY

T. HERBERT BINDLEY, M.A., D.D.

PRINCIPAL OF CODRINGTON COLLEGE, BARBADOS; EXAMINING CHAPLAIN
TO THE LORD BISHOP

PUBLISHED UNDER THE DIRECTION OF THE TRACT COMMITTEE

LONDON:
SOCIETY FOR PROMOTING CHRISTIAN KNOWLEDGE,
NORTHUMBERLAND AVENUE, W.C.; 43, QUEEN VICTORIA STREET, E.C.
BRIGHTON: 129, NORTH STREET.
NEW YORK: EDWIN S. GORHAM.
1904

BV
230
.C9313
2010

In the interest of creating a more extensive selection of rare historical book reprints, we have chosen to reproduce this title even though it may possibly have occasional imperfections such as missing and blurred pages, missing text, poor pictures, markings, dark backgrounds and other reproduction issues beyond our control. Because this work is culturally important, we have made it available as a part of our commitment to protecting, preserving and promoting the world's literature. Thank you for your understanding.

INTRODUCTION

THE little work of St. Cyprian's which is here presented in an English translation is in a very true and real sense an "EARLY CHURCH CLASSIC," for it was early accorded by the Church the position of the recognized standard treatise on the LORD'S PRAYER. So high was the esteem in which it was held that St. Hilary of Poitiers, writing just one hundred years later (A.D. 354), considered himself relieved from the task of commenting on the LORD'S PRAYER when, in the course of his Exposition on St. Matthew, he came to Chapter vi. 9-13, preferring rather to send his readers to St. Cyprian's well-known book.[1]

St. Ambrose, again, in his Commentary on St.

[1] "De orationis autem sacramento necessitate commentandi Cyprianus vir sanctae memoriae liberavit. Quanquam et Tertullianus hinc volumen aptissimum scripserit; sed consequens error hominis detraxit scriptis probabilibus auctoritatem." So St. Hilary. St. Vincent of Lerins has some similar remarks in his Commonitory (chap. xviii.). Some passages from Tertullian's "very appropriate volume" will be found below (pages 71 f.).

Luke, makes no remarks on Chapter xi. 1–4 (the verses containing the LORD'S PRAYER). The value of the work was very fully recognized also by St. Augustine, who read it over to some delegates from the monks at Adrumetum who were inclined to Pelagianism, and strongly recommended the study of it to the monastery, "because it taught that all things which relate to character, whereby we live rightly, are to be asked of Our Father in heaven, and that to presume on the strength of our free-will is to fall from grace."[1]

More than a dozen times in his anti-Pelagian treatises does St. Augustine quote this small work of St. Cyprian, whom he calls "superlatively victorious," because he had anticipatorily refuted heresies as yet unborn.

The scheme of the book, it must be admitted, is borrowed by St. Cyprian from the work on the same subject (*De Oratione*) by his "master" Tertullian. But if Tertullian provided the rough blocks in the quarry, it is St. Cyprian who smoothed and shaped and polished them, adding in almost every case some beautiful thought all his own.[2] And he fortunately avoids both the rugged obliquity of style[3] and diffuseness of treat-

---

[1] Augustine, *Epist.* 215 *ad Valerian*.
[2] The verbal coincidences, not many in number, are collected in Archbishop Benson's *Cyprian*, p. 276.
[3] On the style of St. Cyprian see Watson's essay in

ment which to some extent disfigure Tertullian's tract. Doubtless he lacks both the genius and the passion and the forcefulness of his "master," but the genius was often wayward, the passion fanatical, and the forcefulness overbold. St. Cyprian's gift was to rule, to administer, to interpret; and he remained calm and level-headed in days of pest, of panic, and of persecution, which must have sorely tried his patience and his perseverance.

§ 2. St. Cyprian's Life.

Some slight sketch of St. Cyprian's life must be given here, inasmuch as several points which he emphasizes in his exposition of the LORD'S PRAYER are illuminated by the personality, the character, and the actions of the writer.

This great representative of the Church of Africa —Thascius Caecilius Cyprianus, to give him his full name—was born (not, it would appear, at Karthage) of wealthy parentage in the earlier years of the third century. At the moment when he first comes before us he is the recognized foremost professor of rhetoric in the brilliant pagan society of

---

Studia Biblica, vol. iv. (Oxf. Univ. Press, 1896), and l'Abbé Léonard's edition of four treatises of St. Cyprian (Namur, 1887).

the capital of North Africa.[1] His fortune was large, his position conspicuous, his manner of life free and unrestrained. Yet with all the external ministers to enjoyment around him he felt that "leanness in the soul" to which the nobler pagans invariably, if unconsciously, bear witness. At length he yielded obedience to the inner voice which called him. He entered upon the catechumenate and was prepared for Baptism, "the laver of healing water," by his friend the presbyter Caecilianus. He began at once to practise a large-hearted charity, disposing of some of his estates, and distributing the whole of the proceeds to the poor. He was baptized probably on Easter-eve, A.D. 246. He passed his Diaconate in the house of his spiritual father, Caecilian, having sold his own spacious Gardens in addition to his farms. The Gardens were, however, bought in by friends, but only to be disposed of again at a later time in the same excellent cause. In a year he was admitted to the Presbyterate by the bishop Donatus,[2] A.D. 247; and so marked was his zeal, his devotion, and his splendid capability, that on the death of the Bishop the *vox*

---

[1] Hieronym. *Comm. in Jon.* 3, "in tantam gloriam venit eloquentiae ut oratoriam quoque doceret Carthagini." Cp. *de vir. illustr.* 67. Lactantius speaks to the same effect, *Div. Inst.* v. 1; and Augustine of his trumpet-like voice in forensic contests, *Serm.* 312. 4.

[2] *Ad Donat.* 3, 4.

populi named Cyprian as his successor. " He was the first instance of greater progress being made by faith than by time." " He had as ripe a faith at first as few perhaps have at last." " The Chair of the Episcopate received him such as he was, it did not make his character."[1]

Reluctantly, and not until convinced that it was the will of God,[2] he consented to the call, and was consecrated by the Bishops of the African Province, some time after June A.D. 248, though not without the opposition of a clique of five Presbyters, who maintained an organized hostility towards him for many years.

Not many months of vigorous work passed before the thirty-eight years' peace of the Christians in Africa was rudely broken by the Edict of Decius in January A.D. 249, which visited the Bishops with proscription, imprisonment, banishment, and death.[3] Thus was the first really systematic method of persecution inaugurated. The object which Decius set before himself was the restoration of the old Roman virtue, discipline, and religion, and the extermination of such persons as the Christians, who obstinately refused to fall in with his desire to maintain in renewed integrity the

[1] The above details and some of the phrases are taken from the Life written by his own Deacon Pontius.
[2] *Epist.* 43 ; 59.
[3] *Epist.* 66.

worship of the ancient deities. With true insight he consequently struck first at the Bishops, as the leaders and recognized heads of the organized Christian communities. Amongst others Fabian of Rome, Babylas of Antioch, and Alexander of Jerusalem at once glorified God by their deaths. But although the Bishops alone were named, at Karthage, at any rate, every one who failed to profess Paganism before a certain day stood *ipso facto* a confessed Christian.[1] Tortures were employed to extort a denial of the Faith; many lapsed and many died under the inquisition.

Cyprian himself retired from Karthage in order to maintain the continuity of his episcopal rule.[2] The place of his concealment was known only to those with whom he corresponded. He left large sums in the hands of trustees for the relief of the sufferers,[3] and not only sustained the Church in his own large diocese, but inaugurated that policy towards the lapsed which henceforth became the rule of the West.

Early in the year 251 Decius left Rome to repel the advance of the Goths and to crush the rebel Priscus. With his departure the persecution waned,

[1] *De lapsis* 3.
[2] He based his action on Christ's command, St. Matt. x. 23; *Epist.* 16; *De lapsis* 10.
[3] See an interesting note by Mr. Watson in *J. Theol. Studies*, ii. 433 f.

and finally ceased on his death in November. Cyprian returned to Karthage, and held four Councils, A.D. 251-254, which dealt with matters of great importance, such as the recognition of Cornelius as Bishop of Rome, the schismatic Novatianists, and the treatment of the lapsed. Into these questions it is not necessary for us to enter here.

Meanwhile the Great Plague, which had begun in Æthiopia in the year 250, and had ravaged Ægypt, Syria, and Greece, swept over Africa. It reached Karthage in 252, under the form of a malignant type of fever, and it raged throughout the civilized world for a period of twenty years. Cyprian took the lead in noble measures of relief. Under his inspiriting guidance the Christian body responded to the requirements of its splendid birthright,[1] and cared for, nursed, and buried the sufferers and victims of the foul pestilence without making any distinction between Jew, Pagan, or Christian. While the Christian remedies were practical and sanitary, acompanied by earnest prayers to the Most High, the Pagan course was to multiply sacrifices to the deities of Health, and to issue edicts which once more brought the Christians into disfavour with the panic-stricken populaces. Cyprian was again proscribed, and in 257

[1] "Respondere nos decet natalibus nostris," were Cyprian's stirring words.—Pont. *Vita* 9.

INTRODUCTION

"relegated" to Curubis,[1] a lonely coast town, fifty miles south-east of Karthage—not, however, before he had held further and most important Councils on the Baptismal Question. Happily, the points involved in this controversy do not concern us here.

Already in June, when in the East, the Emperor Valerian had placed in the hands of his Chancellor of the Exchequer, Macrianus, an Edict which separated the Bishops from their flocks, and forbade the Christians to assemble for worship or to enter their cemeteries. In July 258 a much severer Edict was published. It condemned all clergy to death; laics of high rank to degradation and loss of property, or to death if obstinacy were shewn; matrons, *i.e.* wives not in the power (*manus*) of their husbands, to confiscation of goods and exile; and Caesarians[2] to confiscation of goods and labour as chained convicts on the Imperial farms. The Emperor's object evidently was to remove the officials and leading members of the Church, in the hope that thereby the rest would be terrified into

---

[1] Valerian's Edict was dated in July: Cyprian was tried on August 30, and must have left Karthage a little less than a fortnight later, as he reached Curubis on September 14.—Pont. *Vita* 12, 13; Act. Proc. 3, 6.

[2] *Caesariani* were revenue officers under the Chancellor of the Imperial Exchequer. They were employed in matters of escheat and distraint (Hoffman, *Lex. Univ. s.v.*; Codex Justinian. x. 1, 5).

submission, and thus the whole Christian body be reclaimed for Paganism.

While in exile Cyprian largely relieved the sufferers from his own still considerable property, and this fact shows that his high rank, as *vir honestior*, had procured for him the usual exemptions from the stricter penalties of the Edict. On the arrival of the Edict at Karthage the proconsul, Galerius Maximus, summoned Cyprian to appear before him. The year's exile thus ended—but only to be followed by martyrdom. At first Cyprian was bidden to confine himself to his own Gardens at Karthage, for the proconsul lay sick at Utica; but as soon as Galerius came to Karthage the Archbishop's trial was held. He refused to sacrifice, and the inevitable sentence of death was received by the saint with an exclamation of thanksgiving to God. He was led out to the place of execution, but the headsman's hand was unnerved, and the centurion himself was obliged to deliver the stroke. Such was St. Cyprian's "coronation." The date was September the 14th.[1] He stands forth as the first African Bishop "who dyed his sacerdotal diadems in blood."[2]

[1] On the mistake which transferred the festival of St. Cyprian in the English Kalendar to the 26th, see Benson, *u. s.*, pp. 610 f.
[2] Pont. *Vita* 18.

§ 3. THE DATE OF THE TREATISE.

From internal evidence it is clear that Cyprian was writing at a time when it was necessary to emphasize the duty of unity, brotherhood, and unanimity (Chaps. viii., ix., xxiv.), subjects which link this treatise very closely with that "On the Unity of the Church," which was written in A.D. 251. Further, he was writing in the midst of persecution, when martyrdom and confessorship might be every-day occurrences, and when there was a danger of arrogance and self-glorification on the part of the sufferers (Chap. xxvi.). Again, the passages in which he dwells upon the snares of wealth and the duty of dedicating worldly opulence to the cause of God and His saints gain new force when we remember how freely he had surrendered his own property for the relief of the victims of Decius' Edict. Once again, the manner in which he urges the splendid privileges and corresponding duties of Christians as "sons of God," points to the period of the Plague and of his bracing exhortations to the brethren to rise to the opportunity given them of displaying the character of men "born of God" (Chaps. xi., xvii., xxiii.).

All these indications lead us to the year A.D. 252 for the composition of the treatise.

§ 4. CYPRIAN'S TEXT OF THE PATERNOSTER.

PATER NOSTER QUI ES IN CAELIS, SANCTIFICETUR NOMEN TUUM, ADVENIAT REGNUM TUUM, FIAT VOLUNTAS TUA IN CAELO ET IN TERRA, PANEM NOSTRUM COTTIDIANUM DA NOBIS HODIE, ET DIMITTE NOBIS DEBITA NOSTRA, SICUT ET NOS REMITTIMUS DEBITORIBUS NOSTRIS, ET NE PATIARIS NOS INDUCI IN TEMPTATIONEM, SED LIBERA NOS A MALO.[1]

This form of the text is that which was most familiar, probably from its liturgical and devotional

[1] Chap. vii. ; compare Tertullian's text, compiled from the detached clauses in his *De Oratione*:—

PATER QUI IN CAELIS ES, SANCTIFICETUR NOMEN TUUM, FIAT VOLUNTAS TUA IN CAELIS ET IN TERRA, VENIAT REGNUM TUUM, PANEM NOSTRUM QUOTIDIANUM DA NOBIS HODIE, DIMITTE NOBIS DEBITA NOSTRA, . . . NE NOS INDUCAS IN TEMPTATIONEM, SED DEVEHE NOS A MALO.

The omitted clause after NOSTRA seems to be implied by the comment, "remittere nos quoque profitemur debitoribus nostris ;" but the reversed order of the third and fourth clauses is peculiar to Tertullian. For a possible explanation of this order see Chase, "The Lord's Prayer in the Early Church," Cambridge *Texts and Studies*, i. 3. 27.

use, in the North African Church,[1] and the words naturally flowed from the pen or rose to the lips, much as in our own case the English version of the Lord's Prayer in the Prayer Book is the one which we naturally quote and use. Probably very few persons could cite accurately the Biblical text of the Prayer as given in the Authorized Version of either St. Matthew or St. Luke.

Thus both Tertullian and Cyprian read and interpreted the third petition in the form, THY WILL BE DONE IN HEAVEN AND IN EARTH, and Augustine tells us that in his day this form was sometimes preferred, although the other form, AS IN HEAVEN, was more usually used and read in the majority of manuscripts.[2] This form obviously prevented both commentators from finding a model for earthly obedience to God's will in that of the celestial hierarchy or of Nature. IN HEAVEN AND IN EARTH means for Tertullian and for Cyprian either " in the two parts of man's nature, spirit and flesh," or else " in Christians and in unbelievers." Tertullian writes, "By a figurative interpretation

[1] On the "African" text and its close affinity with that of Codex Bobiensis (k) see Sanday, *Old Latin Biblical Texts*, i. 67 ; ii. app. ii.

[2] Augustin. *De dono persev.* iii. 6 : " Tertia petitio est, *Fiat voluntas tua in caelo et in terra :* vel, quod in plerisque codicibus legitur magisque ab orantibus frequentatur, *sicut in caelo et in terra:* quod plerique intellegunt, sicut sancti angeli et nos faciamus voluntatem tuam.

INTRODUCTION

of flesh and spirit we are heaven and earth; although even if it be understood simply, yet the sense of the petition is the same, namely, that in us God's will may be done in earth so that it may also be done in heaven."[1]

And Cyprian similarly, "Since we possess a body from earth and a spirit from heaven we are ourselves earth and heaven, and in both—that is, in body and in spirit—we pray that God's will may be done. . . . We pray also for those who are still earth and who have not begun to be heavenly that, in their case also, the will of God may be done. . . . We make intercession for the salvation of all, so that as in heaven—that is, in us—through our faith God's will has been done, whereby we are of heaven, so also in earth—that is, in those others—God's will may be done, on their becoming believers; so that those who are yet earthly by their first birth, may begin to be heavenly, when born of water and of the Spirit."[2]

Augustine notices these interpretations of his exegetical predecessors and adds to them in his Treatise on the Sermon on the Mount.[3] By "heaven and earth" he understands the righteous and the sinners. "We pray (he says) for our enemies, as though it were said, As the saints do Thy will so also let sinners, that they may be con-

[1] *De Oratione* 4. [2] Chap. xvii., p. 46.
[3] *De Serm. in Monte*, ii. 21 f.

verted unto Thee." And again, following Tertullian's idea, "We understand heaven and earth as spirit and flesh." More boldly he also identifies heaven with Christ and earth with the Church.[1]
It will be observed that in the last petition Cyprian's text differs from Tertullian's, reading DO NOT SUFFER US TO BE LED INTO TEMPTATION. These words are in fact Tertullian's commentary on the clause, and represent the current devotional exposition of the true text, LEAD US NOT INTO TEMPTATION.[2] Referring to this variation Augustine agrees that the petition has no other meaning but " Do not permit us to be led into temptation ; " and adds that for this reason some persons so made their petition, and that it was so read in a considerable number of manuscripts, and that the blessed Cyprian so read it, but that he himself had nowhere found that reading in the original Greek.[3]

[1] "Sicut in Ipso Domino Nostro Jesu Christo ita et in ecclesia."
[2] See below, p. 77. We may add here two other passages to the same effect :— *De fuga in pers.* 2, " Deliver us from the evil one, that is, Do not lead us into temptation by giving us up to the evil one. For then are we delivered from the power of the devil when we are not handed over to him to be tempted." *Adv. Marc.* iv. 26, "Who will suffer us not to be led into temptation ? He Whom the tempter cannot fear, or He Who from the beginning precondemned the tempter ? "
[3] *De dono persever.* vi. 12, " Quod itaque dicimus Deo *Ne nos inferas in tentationem*, quod dicimus nisi ne nos inferri sinas ? Unde sic orant nonnulli et legitur in codicibus

INTRODUCTION 19

This form of the petition in fact first appears in Cyprian, and won its way into some manuscripts from current devotional use.

It is the idea of the Divine permission in temptation that is prominent, derived no doubt from the scenes depicted in the opening chapters of the Book of Job, and verbally indebted to St. Paul's words in 1 Cor. x. 13. Sometimes this last text is combined with 1 Tim. vi. 9, as in a fragment of Dionysius of Alexandria, who explains LEAD US NOT INTO TEMPTATION, that is, "Do not suffer us to fall into temptation."[1] Similarly, some of the early Liturgies added in the embolismus the words, "such as we are not able to bear," from 1 Cor. x. 13.[2] With insertions like these we may compare the liturgical doxology which has wedded itself with the eucharistic employment of the Prayer from very early times.[3]

It may not be out of place to mention here another early variant in the Western text of the Prayer: LET THY HOLY SPIRIT COME UPON US

---

pluribus, et hoc sic posuit beatissimus Cyprianus: *Ne patiaris nos induci in tentationem.* In evangelio tamen graeco nusquam inveni nisi *Ne nos inferas in tentationem.*"
[1] Quoted by Chase, *op. cit.*, pp. 68, 140.
[2] Comp. Liturgy of Alexandria (Brightman, i. 136), Lit. of Syrian Jacobites (*ib.* 100), Lit. of Coptic Jacobites (*ib.* 182).
[3] See Westcott and Hort, *APP., Notes on Select Readings*, Matt. vi. 13; Luke xi. 2; and Chase, *u. s.*, pp. 168 f.

INTRODUCTION

AND CLEANSE US. This is attested by Tertullian[1] and by Gregory Nyssen.[2] It seems to have replaced the clause HALLOWED BE THY NAME, in Tertullian's text, and, THY KINGDOM COME, in Gregory's copies of St. Luke's Gospel. No doubt it was a liturgical addition employed in some services, such as Ordination, when the presence of the Holy Spirit was especially invoked.

§ 5. LITURGICAL ALLUSIONS.

Not the least interesting of the many valuable points in the Treatise are the allusions which it contains to the worship of the North African Church.

1. First in importance amongst these stands the very definite testimony to the Priest's exhortation and the People's response in the Eucharistic Service,[3] which Cyprian quotes in order to illustrate the duty of whole-heartedness in prayer, and of banishing all carnal and worldly thoughts:—

SURSUM CORDA:
HABEMUS AD DOMINUM.

[1] *adv. Marcion.* 26.   [2] *Prec.* 738.
[3] There is a still earlier reference to this formula in the Canons of Hippolytus, which date some thirty years before this Treatise. See Duchesne, *Les Origines du culte chrétien*, p. 506; or, in Mrs. McClure's English translation (S.P.C.K.), p. 526.

It has been suggested [1] that the very ruggedness and abruptness of the Latin point to a still earlier Greek form, like that given in the Syrian rite :

"Ἄνω τὸν νοῦν,

or in Cyril's *Catecheses* (xxiii. 4) :

"Ἄνω τὰς καρδίας,

UP HEARTS!

Habemus ad Dominum is unquestionably a phrase condensed to the point of obscurity. "We hold ourselves," or "We direct (our hearts), towards the Lord," would be the simplest translation. Our familiar English version is taken either from the Mozarabic missal of A.D. 1500—*Levamus ad Dominum*, or from the Cologne "Order" of 1543 —"Wir erheben die zum Herren."

2. In the next place we have to note the incidental allusion to standing as the usual attitude in prayer.[2] The Christian Church inherited this custom from the Jews, and Christ assumed that this would be the ordinary practice of His followers, even when praying for the pardon ot sins.[3] So the Pharisee and the Tax-gatherer are both depicted in the parable as standing to pray.[4]

[1] Bishop Dowden's *Workmanship of the Prayer-Book*, p. 168.
[2] Chap. xxxi.   [3] Mark xi. 25 : chap. xxiii.
[4] Luke xviii. 10 f. : chap. vi.

"This posture was made obligatory, by custom, during the festal Easter season, and also on Sunday, as symbolizing the participation of the redeemed in the risen life of their Redeemer, and expressing the erectness and jubilance and deathless expectation which were inseparable from the commemoration of His victory over death."[1] One is tempted to quote Clement of Alexandria:— "Prayer is converse with God. . . . Herein we raise the head and lift the hands towards heaven, and stand on tiptoe as we join in the closing outburst of prayer, following the eager flight of the spirit into the intelligible world: and while we thus endeavour to detach the body from the earth by uplifting it along with the uttered words, we spurn the fetters of the flesh and constrain the soul, winged with desire of better things, to ascend into the holy place."[2]

3. The third point to notice is Cyprian's clear indication that the Holy Eucharist was received daily.[3] This was a common, but by no means an invariable custom. Tertullian speaks of the fourth

---

[1] Bright, *Notes on the Canons*, p. 83. Comp. Tertullian's words, *De cor.* 3, "On the Lord's Day we account it unlawful to fast or to worship upon the knees. We enjoy the same freedom from Easter Day to Pentecost"; and, further, *De Oratione* 23.

[2] *Strom.* vii. 39, 40 (Hort and Mayor ed., p. 69).

[3] Chap. xviii.

INTRODUCTION 23

and sixth days (Wednesdays and Fridays) as "station-days" when the Communion was administered.[1] But later, in Augustine's time, the daily celebration was observed, presumably in the chief church in Hippo, though varying customs prevailed elsewhere.[2] The daily reception was encouraged by the practice of allowing communicants to take home with them certain reserved portions of the consecrated elements, to be partaken of on arising in the morning before all other food.[3]

4. On the observance of the Three Hours of Prayer—the third, the sixth, and the ninth—Cyprian offers a mystical explanation, with which we may compare that given by Clement of Alexandria. Clement writes:[4] "If there are any who assign fixed hours to prayer, such as the third, the sixth, and the ninth . . . the triple distribution of the hours and their observance by corresponding prayers is familiar to those who are acquainted with the blessed triad of the holy mansions."

But Cyprian evidently had in mind the words of his master Tertullian, who speaks of these Three Hours as "having always been of special solemnity in prayer."[5] On the other hand, the

[1] *De Oratione* 14.
[2] Augustin., *Epist.* 98. 9 : 118 *ad Jan.*
[3] Tertullian, *Ad uxor.* 5 ; Cyprian, *De laps.* 26.
[4] *Strom.* vii. 40.
[5] *De jejun.* 10 ; comp. Origen, *De Oratione* 12.

hidden symbolism of the Holy Trinity is entirely Cyprianesque.

* * * * *

We have kept the reader from the text of this beautiful little work too long.

ST. CYPRIAN ON THE LORD'S PRAYER

CHAPTER I

THE Gospel precepts, dearly beloved brethren, are nothing else than divine commands, foundations on which hope is to be built up, buttresses by which faith is to be strengthened, nourishment wherefrom the heart is to be comforted, helms whereby to steer our way, ramparts whereby salvation is to be preserved; and thus, while they instruct the teachable minds of believers on earth, they also lead them on to the heavenly kingdom.

There are many things which God willed should be proclaimed and made known by His servants the Prophets, but how much more important are those which His Son speaks, which the Word of God Who was in the Prophets testifies with His own voice; not now demanding that the way should be prepared for His coming, but coming Himself, opening and shewing a way for us, so that we, who were formerly recklessly and blindly wandering *in the darkness of death*,[1] might, when

[1] Luke i. 79.

illuminated by the light of grace, hold to the way of life with the Lord as our Guide and Ruler.

CHAPTER II

THE Lord, amongst other saving warnings and divine precepts with which He gave counsel for the salvation of His people, Himself gave also a form of prayer, and Himself taught and instructed us for what we should pray. He Who made us to live taught us also to pray, moved by that same lovingkindness wherewith He has deigned also to grant and confer all things else; so that when we speak in the presence of the Father, with the petition and prayer which His Son taught, we shall be heard the more readily.

Already He had foretold that the hour was coming when the *true worshippers* would *worship the Father in spirit and in truth;*[1] and now He fulfilled what He then promised, in order that we, who have been receivers of spirit and truth through the sanctification which He gives, may worship Him truly and spiritually by using that which He has delivered.

For what prayer can be more spiritual than that

[1] John iv. 23.

THE LORD'S PRAYER

which has been given us by Christ, by Whom also the Holy Spirit was sent to us? What praying in the presence of the Father can be more true than that which was delivered by the lips of the Son Who is *the Truth?*[1] Hence to pray otherwise than He taught is not merely ignorance but a fault; for He Himself ruled and said, "Ye reject the commandment of God in order to observe your own tradition."[2]

CHAPTER III

LET us pray therefore, dearly beloved brethren, as our Master, God, hath taught us. It is a loving and familiar thing to beseech God with His own petitioning and to ascend to Him with the prayer of Christ. Let the Father recognize the words of His own Son when we make our requests. Let Him Who dwells within our breast be also in our voice; and inasmuch as we have Him as *an Advocate with the Father*[3] for our sins, when as

[1] John xiv. 6.   [2] Mark vii. 8.   [3] 1 John ii. 1.

Compare Wordsworth's Sonnet, from the Italian of Michael Angelo:

To the SUPREME BEING.

"The prayers I make will then be sweet indeed
If Thou the spirit give by which I pray."

sinners we seek pardon for our delinquencies, let us put forward the words of our *Advocate*. For as He says that whatsoever we ask from the Father in His Name He will give us,[1] how much more unfailingly shall we obtain what we ask in Christ's Name if we ask it in His own words.

CHAPTER IV

BUT let our words of prayer be under strict rule, restrained by quietness and modesty. Let us recollect that we stand in the sight of God. The Divine Eyes must be pleased with the posture of our body and the tone of our voice. For as a shameless man will shout with loud cries, so on the other hand it becomes a reverent man to pray with modest prayers. Moreover, the Lord in His directions bade us pray in secret, in secluded and sequestered places, in our very chambers,[2] as best suited to faith, so that we may recognize that God is everywhere present, hearing and seeing every one, and, in the plenitude of His Majesty, penetrating even into secluded and hidden places, as it is written:[3] *I am a God nigh at hand, and not a God afar off. If a man shall hide himself in secret places, shall I therefore not see him? Do I not fill*

[1] John xvi. 23.   [2] Matt. vi. 6.   [3] Jerem. xxiii. 23 f.

THE LORD'S PRAYER

heaven and earth? And again: *In every place the eyes of God behold the good and the wicked.*[1]

And when we come together into one place with the brethren and celebrate divine sacrifices with God's priest, we ought to be mindful of reverence and order, not tossing our prayers into the air on all sides with ill-assorted words, nor flinging out a petition, which ought to be modestly commended to God, with tumultuous loquacity, because God is the Hearer not of the voice but of the heart. Nor does He Who sees the thoughts need to be reminded by loud cries. This the Lord shews, when He says: *Why think ye evil in your hearts?*[2] And in another place: *And all the churches shall know that I am a searcher of the reins and heart.*[3]

CHAPTER V

THIS rule Anna, in the first Book of Kings, preserves and keeps, betokening a type of the Church, in that she was praying to the Lord not with clamorous petitioning, but silently and modestly within the very recesses of her breast. She was speaking with secret prayer but with manifest faith; she was speaking not with her voice but with her heart, because she knew that

[1] Prov. xv. 3.   [2] Luke v. 22.   [3] Rev. ii. 23.

God so hears; and she gained her petition effectually because she sought it faithfully. Divine Scripture declares this, saying: *She was speaking in her heart, and her lips moved, and her voice was not heard; and God heard her.*[1]

Also we read in the Psalms: *Speak in your hearts and on your beds, and be filled with compunction.*[2]

By Jeremiah also the Holy Spirit suggests the same and teaches us, saying: *In the heart, O God, it is due to Thee to be worshipped.*[3]

CHAPTER VI

MOREOVER, let not the worshipper, dearly beloved brethren, forget the manner in which the tax-gatherer prayed in the temple with the Pharisee. Not with eyes presumptuously raised to heaven, not with hands proudly held aloft, but beating upon his breast and testifying to the sins therein inclosed, he implored help from the Divine mercy. And while the Pharisee was self-contented, it was the rather granted to this

[1] 1 Sam. i. 13.   [2] Psalm iv. 4.
[3] *Epist. Jerem. apud* Baruch vi. 6. In the original context the meaning is quite different. The contrast emphasized by Jeremiah is not that between the heart and the lips, but between the worship of God and the worship of the Babylonian idols.

other man who thus prayed, to be sanctified, inasmuch as he placed his hope of salvation, not in reliance on his own innocence (for no one is innocent), but prayed, humbly confessing his sins. And He Who pardons the humble heard his prayer. This the Lord sets forth in His Gospel, and says:[1] *Two men went up into the temple to pray, one a Pharisee and one a tax-gatherer. The Pharisee, when he had placed himself, prayed thus with himself: "God, I thank Thee that I am not as other men, unjust, extortioners, adulterers, even as this tax-gatherer. I fast twice in the week; I give tithes of all that I possess." But the tax-gatherer was standing far away, and was not even willing to lift his eyes unto heaven, but kept smiting upon his breast, saying, " God, be merciful to me, a sinner." I tell you that this man went down to his house justified rather than that Pharisee. For every one that exalteth himself shall be humbled, and he that humbleth himself shall be exalted.*[2]

[1] Luke xviii. 10 f.
[2] One cannot forbear quoting Crashaw's epigram :—
"Two went to pray? O rather say
One went to brag, th' other to pray.

One stands up close, and treads on high,
Where th' other dares not lend his eye.

One nearer to the altar trod,
The other to the altar's God."

CHAPTER VII

THESE things, dearly beloved brethren, we learn from the sacred lection. And now, after we have learnt how we ought to enter upon prayer, let us learn also what we are to pray, the Lord being our Teacher. *After this manner*, said He,[1] *pray ye:*

OUR FATHER WHO ART IN HEAVEN, HALLOWED BE THY NAME, THY KINGDOM COME, THY WILL BE DONE IN HEAVEN AND IN EARTH. GIVE US THIS DAY OUR DAILY BREAD, AND FORGIVE US OUR DEBTS AS WE ALSO FORGIVE OUR DEBTORS. AND SUFFER US NOT TO BE LED INTO TEMPTATION, BUT DELIVER US FROM THE EVIL ONE. AMEN.

CHAPTER VIII

BEFORE all things the Teacher of peace and Master of unity is unwilling for prayer to be made singly and individually, teaching that he who prays is not to pray for himself alone. For we do not say, *My Father Who art in heaven*, nor *Give me this day my bread*, nor does each one ask

[1] Matt. vi. 9.

THE LORD'S PRAYER 33

that his own debt only be remitted, nor does he request for himself alone that he may not be led into temptation and may be delivered from the evil one. Prayer with us is public and common; and when we pray we do not pray for one but for the whole people, because we the whole people are one.

The God of peace and Master of concord Who taught unity thus wished one to pray for all, as He Himself bore all in One. This rule of prayer the Three Children observed when shut up in the furnace of fire, for they were in unison in prayer and concordant in unanimity of spirit. Which fact the truth of the sacred Scriptures declareth; and when it teaches how such persons prayed, it gives us an example which we ought to imitate in our prayers, that we may be like them. *Then those three*, it says,[1] *as if from one mouth sang a hymn and blessed the Lord.* They spake as if from one mouth, although Christ had not yet taught them to pray. And therefore, as they prayed, their words were availing and efficacious, because a quiet, simple, and spiritual prayer pleased the Lord.

Thus too we find that the Apostles and disciples prayed after the Lord's Ascension: *They all continued with one accord in prayer, with*

[1] Song of the Three Holy Children, verse 28 [Daniel iii. 51].

34 ST. CYPRIAN ON

the women, and Mary the Mother of Jesus, and with His brethren.[1] They continued with one accord in prayer, clearly shewing at once by the constancy of their prayer and by its unanimity that God, *Who maketh men to be of one mind in an house,*[2] only admits into the divine and eternal house those among whom prayer is unanimous.

CHAPTER IX

Now see what kind of lessons are to be learnt, dearly beloved brethren, from the Lord's Prayer! how numerous, how important! briefly bound together in words, yet spiritually abounding in virtue! so much so that there is absolutely nothing passed over pertaining to our petitions and prayers which is not included in this compendium of heavenly teaching.

After this manner, saith He, *pray ye:*

OUR FATHER WHO ART IN HEAVEN.

The new man, born again, and restored to his God by His grace, says first of all FATHER, because he now has begun to be a son.

He came, the Gospel says,[3] *to His own home and*

---

[1] Acts i. 14.   [2] Psalm lxvii. 7. [lxviii. 6.]
[3] John i. 11.

THE LORD'S PRAYER

His own people received Him not. But to as many as received Him He gave power to become sons of God, namely to those who believe in His Name. He therefore who has believed in His Name and has become a son of God ought at once to begin to give thanks and to proclaim himself a son of God by declaring that he has a Father in Heaven, God. Let him witness too among the very first words of his (new) birth that he has renounced his earthly and fleshly father, and that he recognizes and has begun to have as his Father only Him Who is in heaven; as it is written: [1] *They who say to father and to mother, I have not known thee, and who have acknowledged their own children, these have guarded Thy precepts and observed Thy covenant.*

Likewise the Lord in His Gospel[2] forbids us to call anyone "*father*" *on earth*, because we have *One Father, Who is in heaven.* And to the disciple who mentioned his deceased father He replied:[3] *Let the dead bury their dead.* For the man had spoken of his father as dead when the Father of all believers is living.

CHAPTER X

NOR ought we, dearly beloved brethren, merely to consider and understand that we call Him

[1] Deut. xxxiii. 9. [2] Matt. xxiii. 8. [3] Matt. viii. 22.

FATHER, *Who is in heaven*, but we join together and say OUR FATHER; the Father, that is, of those who believe, of those who, sanctified by Him and renewed by the birth of spiritual grace, have begun to be sons of God.

This word, too, censures and lashes the Jews, who not only in their unbelief despised the Christ Who had been foretold to them by the Prophets, and was sent first to them, but also cruelly put Him to death; and they cannot now call God their Father, because the Lord confounds and refutes them, saying:[1] *Ye were born of your father the devil, and the lusts of your father ye are willing to do. For he was a murderer from the beginning, and stood not in the truth, because truth is not in him.* Also by Isaiah the Prophet God cries in wrath:[2] *I have begotten and brought up sons, but they have despised Me. The ox knoweth his owner and the ass his master's crib; but Israel hath not known Me, and My people hath not understood Me. Ah! sinful nation, a people full of sins, a worthless seed, abominable sons. Ye have forsaken the Lord and provoked to indignation the Holy One of Israel.*

In reprobation of these Jews we Christians, when we pray, say OUR FATHER, because He has begun to be ours and has ceased to be the Father of the Jews who have forsaken Him. Nor can a sinful

[1] John viii. 44.   [2] Isaiah i. 3 f.

people be a son; it is to those to whom remission of sins is granted that the name of sons is ascribed, and to them eternity is promised; the Lord Himself saying : [1] *Whosoever committeth sin is the slave of sin. Now a slave doth not abide in the house for ever, but a son abideth for ever.*

CHAPTER XI

Now how great is the Lord's tenderness, how great the exceeding abundance of His condescension and goodness towards us, seeing that He wished us to pray to God in such a manner as to call Him FATHER; and since Christ is Son of God, so may we call ourselves sons of God. For not one of us would have dared to aspire unto this title in prayer had not He Himself permitted us so to pray. We ought then, dearly beloved brethren, to remember and to realize that when we call God FATHER, we ought to act as sons of God, in order that, as we are pleased at God being our Father, so He, too, may be pleased with us. Let us behave as temples of God, so that it may appear that God dwelleth in us. Let not our conduct fall away from the Spirit, but let us who have begun to be heavenly and spiritual

[1] John viii. 34.

ponder and perform naught but heavenly and spiritual things; for the Lord God Himself hath said :[1] *Them that honour Me I will honour, and he that despiseth Me shall be despised.* The blessed Apostle likewise in his Epistle hath ruled :[2] *Ye are not your own. For ye have been bought with a great price. Honour and bear about God in your body.*

CHAPTER XII

AFTER this we say HALLOWED BE THY NAME. Not that we ask for God that He may be hallowed in our prayers, but that we beseech Him that His Name may be hallowed in us. By whom, indeed, could God be hallowed Who is Himself the Hallower? Yet because He Himself has said,[3] *Be ye holy, for I also am holy,* this is what we ask and request; namely, that we who have been hallowed in Baptism may be constant in that which we have begun to be. And for this we make daily supplication. For we need a daily sanctification, whereby we who daily commit faults may purge away our

---

[1] 1 Sam. ii. 30.   [2] 1 Cor. vi. 20.
[3] Luke xx. 7. Comp. 1 Pet. i. 16.

offences by a continual sanctification.[1] Now what that sanctification is which is conferred upon us by the lovingkindness of God the Apostle declares when he says :[2] *Neither fornicators, nor idolaters, nor adulterers, nor effeminate, nor seekers after males, nor thieves, nor cheats, nor drunkards, nor revilers, nor extortioners, shall attain to the kingdom of God. And these, indeed, were ye ; but ye were washed, ye were justified, ye were sanctified in the Name of our Lord Jesus Christ and in the Spirit of our God.*

He says that we were sanctified in the Name of the Lord Jesus Christ and in the Spirit of our God. It is this sanctification that we pray may abide in us. And because our Lord and Judge warns [3] the one who had been healed by Him and granted a new life to *sin no more, lest a worse thing come upon* him, we ask with continual prayers and request that the sanctification and renewed life which is received by God's grace may be preserved by His protecting care.

[1] On the efficacy of the Lord's Prayer as a daily absolution see Augustine, *De civ. Dei*, xxi. 27: "The daily prayer which the Lord Himself taught obliterates the sins of the day, when day by day we say, Forgive us our debts." And again, *Serm. ad Catech.* xv., "Semel abluimus baptismate, cottidie abluimus oratione."

[2] 1 Cor. vi. 9.   [3] John v. 14.

CHAPTER XIII

IT follows in the Prayer, THY KINGDOM COME. We ask that God's kingdom may be made present to us in the same way that we entreat that His Name may be hallowed in us. For when does God not reign? or when begins with Him that which ever was and ever will be?

We ask for our kingdom to come which has been promised to us by God and won by Christ's Blood and Passion; so that we who have already served Him in the world may hereafter reign with Christ the Lord; as He Himself promises when He says:[1] *Come, ye blessed of My Father, receive the kingdom prepared for you from the beginning of the world.*

The kingdom of God, dearly beloved brethren, may also be interpreted of Christ Himself Whom we daily desire to come, and for Whose Advent we pray, that it may quickly be made present to us. For as He is the Resurrection, because we rise in Him, so also He may be regarded as the Kingdom of God, because we are destined to reign in Him.

Now it is well for us to pray for God's kingdom, that is, a heavenly kingdom, because there is also an earthly kingdom. But he who has already renounced the world is superior both to its honours

[1] Matt. xxv. 34.

THE LORD'S PRAYER

and to its kingdom. And so he who dedicates himself to God and Christ longs not for earthly kingdoms but heavenly. But there is need of continual supplication and prayer lest we fall from that heavenly kingdom, as the Jews fell to whom it had first been promised, as the Lord showed and taught. *Many*, saith He,[1] *shall come from the east and from the west and shall sit down with Abraham and Isaac and Jacob in the kingdom of heaven. But the sons of the kingdom shall be expelled into outer darkness; there shall be weeping and gnashing of teeth.* He points out that the Jews were originally the sons of the kingdom when they persevered in being such, but after that the Paternal Name ceased amongst them the kingdom ceased likewise. And hence we Christians, who begin in prayer to call God FATHER, also pray that His kingdom may come to us.

CHAPTER XIV

WE also proceed to say, THY WILL BE DONE IN HEAVEN AND IN EARTH; not meaning that God may do His own will, but that we may be able to do what God wills. For who opposes God

[1] Matt. viii. 11.

so as to prevent Him from doing as He wills? But since we are opposed by the devil, and our own mind and actions hindered in every way from being in submission to God, we ask and beseech that God's will may be done in us. And that it may be done in us, there is need of God's will, that is, of His aid and protecting care, because no one is strong by his own strength, but is secure only by the kindness and mercy of God.

Accordingly even the Lord, manifesting the weakness of that human nature which He bore, says:[1] *Father, if it be possible, let this cup pass from Me.* And then, affording an example to His disciples not to do their own will but God's, He added: *Nevertheless, not what I will, but what Thou wilt.* And in another place He says:[2] *I came down from heaven not to do My own will, but the will of Him that sent Me.* Now if the Son was obedient to do His Father's will, how much more ought the servant to be obedient to do his Lord's will? as John in his Epistle exhorts us to do the will of God, and instructs us, saying:[3] *Love not the world, neither the things that are in the world. If any one love the world the love of the Father is not in him. For all that is in the world is lust of the flesh, and lust of the eyes, and pride of life, which is not from the Father, but is of the world. And the world will*

[1] Matt. xxvi. 39.   [2] John vi. 38.
[3] 1 John ii. 15.

pass away and the lust thereof; but he who hath done the will of God abideth for ever, even as God also abideth for ever.
We who wish to abide for ever ought to do the will of God Who is for ever.

CHAPTER XV

Now the will of God is that which Christ did and taught. It is humility in conduct, stability in faith, modesty in words, justice in deeds, mercy in works, strictness in morals, unwillingness to do wrong, and willingness to endure wrong: it is to preserve peace with our brethren, to love God with our whole heart, to have affection for Him as our Father, to fear Him as our God, to prefer nothing before Christ because He preferred nothing before us, to cling inseparably to His love, to stand bravely and faithfully by His Cross, and when the contest comes for His Name and Honour, to shew forth in speech a constancy whereby we become confessors, in torture a fidelity whereby we defy the foe, and in death a patience wherefor we receive the crown. This it is to endeavour to be co-heir with Christ, this it is to do the will of God, this it is to fulfil the will of the Father.

CHAPTER XVI

MOREOVER we pray that the will of God may be done both in heaven and in earth, because each pertains to the consummation of our safety and salvation. For since we possess a body from earth and a spirit from heaven, we are ourselves earth and heaven; and in both—that is, in body and in spirit—we pray that God's will may be done. For there is a strife between flesh and spirit, a daily contest as they mutually disagree, so that we do not do the things that we would; because while the spirit seeks what is heavenly and divine, the flesh desires what is earthly and worldly. And therefore we pray that by the assistance and help of God there may be agreement between these two; so that when the will of God is done both in the spirit and in the flesh, the soul which has been reborn through Him may be preserved. This is what the Apostle Paul openly and plainly declares in his words:[1] *The flesh lusteth against the Spirit and the Spirit against the flesh, for these are contrary to one another, so that we do not do the things that we would. Now the works of the flesh are manifest, namely, adulteries, fornications, uncleannesses, filthinesses, idolatries, poisonings, murders, enmities*

[1] Gal. v. 17.

THE LORD'S PRAYER 45

strifes, rivalries, hatreds, provocations, jealousies, dissensions, parties, envyings, drunkennesses, revelries, and the like: and those who do such things will not inherit the kingdom of God. But the fruit of the Spirit is love, joy, peace, magnanimity, goodness, faith, gentleness, continence, chastity. And therefore we pray with daily, nay with incessant supplication, that both in heaven and in earth God's will may be done concerning us; because this is the will of God, that the earthly should yield to the heavenly, that the spiritual and divine should prevail.

CHAPTER XVII

AGAIN, it may be understood thus also, dearly beloved brethren, that, as the Lord commanded [1] and admonished us to love even our enemies and to pray likewise for those who persecute us, so we pray also for those who are still earth and who have not begun to be heavenly, that concerning them also the will of God may be done which Christ fulfilled by saving and renewing human nature. For as the disciples are called by Him no longer earth but *the salt of the earth*,[2] and the Apostle says [3] that *the first man is from the dust of*

[1] Matt. v. 44.   [2] Matt. v. 13.   [3] 1 Cor. xv. 47.

the earth, but *the Second Man is from heaven*, rightly do we also, who ought to be like God our Father, Who makes *His sun to rise on the good and on the evil, and sends rain upon the just and the unjust*,[1] pray according to Christ's admonition, and make intercession of all; to the end that as in heaven— that is, in us—through our faith God's will has been done, whereby we are of heaven, so also in earth— that is, in those others—God's will may be done, by their becoming believers. So that those who are yet earthly by their first birth, may begin to be heavenly, *born of water and of the Spirit*.[2]

CHAPTER XVIII

PROCEEDING with the Prayer we make the request: GIVE US THIS DAY OUR DAILY BREAD.

This may be understood both spiritually and literally, since each interpretation by its divine usefulness conduces to our salvation. For Christ is the Bread of Life;[3] and this Bread is not every one's, but is ours. And as we say OUR FATHER, because He is the Father of those who know Him and believe, so also we call it OUR BREAD, because Christ is the Bread of those who partake of His

[1] Matt. v. 45. [2] John iii. 5.
[3] John vi. 48.

Body. Now we request that this Bread be given to us daily lest we, who are in Christ, and who daily receive His Eucharist for food of salvation, should, by the interposition of some heinous crime, be withheld from communion and forbidden the heavenly food, and so be separated from the Body of Christ. This He Himself taught, saying :[1] *I am the Bread of Life, which came down from heaven. If any one eat of My Bread he shall live for ever. Now the Bread which I will give is My Flesh for the life of the world.* Since therefore He says that if any one eat of His Bread he shall live for ever, as it is manifest that there are those living who appertain to His Body and receive the Eucharist by right of communion, so on the other hand we are bound to fear and pray lest any one, being withheld from communion and separated from Christ's Body, remain far from salvation; according to His warning,[2] *Unless ye eat the Flesh of the Son of Man and drink His Blood ye will not have life in you.*

Consequently we pray that OUR BREAD, that is, Christ, may be given to us DAILY, so that we who abide and live in Christ may not fall away from His sanctification and His Body.

[1] John vi. 51.   [2] John vi. 53.

CHAPTER XIX

AGAIN, the petition may also be understood in this way, namely, that we who have renounced the world and rejected its riches and pomps through the faith of a spiritual grace, should ask for ourselves only food and sustenance; as the Lord instructed us, saying:[1] *He who doth not renounce everything that is his cannot be My disciple.* Now he who has begun to be a disciple of Christ, renouncing everything according to his Master's words, ought to ask only for his daily food, and not to extend the desires expressed in his prayers into the future; as once again the Lord Himself prescribes:[2] *Take no thought for the morrow, for the morrow will take thought for itself. Sufficient unto the day is the evil thereof.* Very properly, therefore, doth Christ's disciple ask for sustenance for himself from day to day, since he is forbidden to take thought for the morrow.

Further, it would be an inconsistent and contradictory thing for us, who pray for God's kingdom to come quickly, to ask to live long in the world. Thus also the blessed Apostle admonishes us, substantiating and strengthening the stedfastness of our hope and faith. *We brought nothing into this*

[1] Luke xiv. 33.   [2] Matt. vi. 34.

world, saith he,[1] *and it is certain that we can carry nothing away. Having therefore food and raiment we are content therewith. But those who wish to become rich fall into temptation and snares, and many and hurtful desires, which drown men in perdition and ruin. For a root of all evils is cupidity; which some assiduously seeking have suffered shipwreck from the faith, and have involved themselves in many sorrows.*

CHAPTER XX

HE teaches us that riches are not merely despicable but dangerous, that therein lies the root of seductive evils which deceive the blindness of the human heart by their hidden falsity. Wherefore God found the rich fool guilty, as he was meditating upon his worldly opulence and boasting of the profusion of his abundant harvests, saying:[2] *Thou fool, this night thy soul is required of thee. Whose then will be the things which thou hast provided?* The fool was rejoicing over his harvests on the very night that he was about to die, and he to whom life was now wanting, was thinking of the abundance of his provisions. In opposition to this

[1] 1 Tim. vi. 7.   [2] Luke xii. 20.

the Lord teaches us[1] that he becomes perfect and complete who, by selling all that he has and distributing it for the use of the poor, lays up for himself *treasure in heaven*. He says that that man is able to follow Him and to imitate the glory of the Lord's Passion who, unimpeded and close-girt, is involved in no snare of property, but, himself unrestricted and free, accompanies his own possessions which he has already sent before to God. In order that each one of us may prepare himself for this, he thus learns to pray, and from the terms of the prayer to know what manner of man he ought to be.

CHAPTER XXI

For the just man cannot fail of his daily food, since it is written:[2] *The Lord will not slay the just soul by hunger.* And again:[3] *I have been young and now am old, yet have I not seen the just forsaken, nor his seed begging their bread.* Likewise the Lord promises:[4] *Take no thought saying, What shall we eat or what shall we drink, or wherewithal shall we be clothed? for these things the nations seek*

---

[1] Matt. xix. 21.   [2] Prov. x. 3.
[3] Ps. xxxvi. 25. [xxxvii. 25.]   [4] Matt. vi. 31.

THE LORD'S PRAYER 51

after. But your Father knoweth that ye need all these things. Seek ye first the kingdom and righteousness of God, and all these things shall be added unto you. He promises that all things shall be added to those who seek God's kingdom and righteousness. For since all things are of God, to one who has God nothing will be wanting, if he himself is not wanting towards God.

It was thus that Daniel, when he was shut up in the lions' den by the king's command, was divinely provided with a meal, and the man of God was fed in the midst of hungry yet abstaining wild beasts. Thus was Elijah sustained in his flight, and nourished during persecution by ravens ministering to him in his solitude and birds bringing him food. And—O the detestable cruelty of human malice!—wild beasts spare, birds bring food, and men lay snares and savagely attack!

CHAPTER XXII

AFTER this we proceed to make request regarding our sins, saying : AND FORGIVE US OUR DEBTS AS WE ALSO FORGIVE OUR DEBTORS.

After the supply of food, pardon of sin is asked for, in order that he who is fed by God may live in

God; and that provision be made not only for the present and temporal life, but also for the eternal, whereunto we may come if our sins are pardoned, —sins which the Lord calls OUR DEBTS, as He says in His Gospel, *I forgave thee all thy debt because thou desiredst Me.*[1]

How necessarily, how prudently, and how salutarily are we admonished that we are sinners by being compelled to make petition for our sins, so that while forgiveness is asked of God the mind is recalled to a sense of its guilt! Lest any one should be self-satisfied as though innocent, and by extolling himself should meet with the worse doom, he is instructed and taught that he sins daily, so long as he is bidden daily to entreat for his sins. Thus, for instance, John also in his Epistle warns us, saying:[2] *If we say that we have no sin we deceive ourselves and the truth is not in us; but if we have made confession of our sins, the Lord is faithful and just to forgive us our sins.*

In his Epistle he has embraced both parts, namely, that we ought to make request for our sins, and that we shall obtain pardon when we ask. Hence he said that the Lord was faithful to forgive our sins, maintaining the fidelity of His promise; because He Who has taught us to pray for our debts and sins has promised that the Father's mercy and pardon shall follow.

[1] Matt. xviii. 32.   [2] 1 John i. 8.

CHAPTER XXIII

HE plainly added and laid down the rule, binding us by a definite condition and stipulation, that we should so entreat for our debts to be forgiven according as we ourselves forgive our debtors; knowing that what we ask on behalf of our sins cannot be obtained unless we ourselves have acted in a similar way towards those who have sinned against us. Therefore He says in another place :[1] *With what manner ye shall have meted, it shall be meted out to you again.* And the servant who, after having been forgiven by his lord all that he owed, refused to forgive his fellow-servant, is cast into prison.[2] Because he would not treat with forbearance his fellow-servant he forfeited the forbearance with which he had been treated by his lord. This truth Christ sets forth still more strongly in His injunctions, and deepened in force by His judicial strictness : *When ye stand at prayer,* He says,[3] *forgive if ye have aught against any; so that your Father Who is in heaven may also forgive your sins. But if ye forgive not, neither will your Father Who is in heaven forgive your sins.* No excuse will remain to you in the day of judgment, when you will be judged according to your sentence, and whatever you have done, that also your-

[1] Matt. vii. 2. [2] Matt. xviii. 34. [3] Mark xi. 25.

self will suffer. For God commanded us to be peace-makers, and at concord and of one mind in His house; and such as He makes us by our second birth, that He wishes us when re-born to continue; so that we who are sons of God may remain in the peace of God, and having *One Spirit*[1] may have also one mind and heart. Thus God doth not receive the sacrifice of one in enmity, but bids him return from the altar and first be reconciled to his brother, so that God may be appeased by the prayers of a peace-maker.[2] This is the greater sacrifice before God,—our peace and brotherly concord,—a people joined together through the unity of the Father, and of the Son, and of the Holy Spirit.

CHAPTER XXIV

FOR even in the case of the sacrifices which Cain and Abel were the first to offer, God regarded not their gifts, but their hearts, so that that one was accepted in his gift who was acceptable in his heart. Abel, peaceable and just, sacrificing to God in his innocency, taught others also, when they offer their gifts at the altar, to come with the fear of God, with simplicity of heart, with the principle

---

[1] Eph. iv. 4.   [2] Matt. v. 24.

of justice, with the peace of concord. Deservedly did he who bore that character in his sacrifice to God, himself afterwards become a sacrifice to God; so that he who had had the Lord's righteousness and peace should be the first to shew the example of martyrdom and begin the Lord's Passion by the glory of his blood. Such men are accordingly crowned by the Lord, such will be *avenged*[1] in the day of judgment with the Lord.

But the one who is quarrelsome and he that is at enmity and not at peace with the brethren, as the blessed Apostle and Holy Scripture testify, will not be able to escape from the charge of fraternal dissension, even if he should be slain for the Name (of Christ), because, as it is written,[2] *He who hateth his brother is a murderer;* nor does a murderer attain to the kingdom of heaven or live with God. He cannot be with Christ who hath preferred to imitate Judas rather than Christ. How heinous the sin which not even the Baptism of blood[3] can wash out! How deep the offence which not even martyrdom can expiate!

[1] *Vindicabuntur:* compare Rev. vi. 10; but another reading is *judicabunt,* " will judge."
[2] 1 John iii. 15.
[3] On the efficacy of Martyrdom for the pardon of sins see Tertullian, *Apol.* 50, *de pat.* 13, *de bapt.* 16. He terms it "a second Baptism."

CHAPTER XXV

FURTHERMORE the Lord needfully admonishes us to say in the Prayer, AND SUFFER US NOT TO BE LED INTO TEMPTATION. Hereby it is shewn that the adversary can avail nothing against us unless God previously give him permission; so that all our fear and devotion and heedfulness should be turned towards God, since in our temptations no power is allowed to the evil one save that which is derived from God. Scripture proves this when it records[1] that *Nebuchadnezzar, king of Babylon, came against Jerusalem and stormed it, and the Lord delivered it into his hand.* Now power is given to the evil one against us according to our sins, as it is written:[2] *Who gave Jacob for a spoil and Israel to those that plundered him? Did not the Lord, against Whom they sinned, and refused to walk in His ways and to hear His law? And He hath poured upon them the fury of His anger.* And again, when Solomon sinned and fell away from the commandments and ways of the Lord, it is recorded:[3] *And the Lord stirred up Satan against Solomon.*

[1] 2 Kings xxiv. 11.   [2] Isaiah xlii. 25.
[3] 1 Kings xi. 14. But the Hebrew word for Satan, which is merely transliterated by the LXX. and old Latin, is not in this passage used as a proper name to denote the personal devil, but simply for an adversary.

CHAPTER XXVI

IN truth, power is given to be used against us for a twofold purpose—for punishment when we sin, and for glory when we are proved; as we see in the case of Job, for God makes this clear, saying:[1] *Beho'd, all that he hath I give into thy hands; but beware that thou touch not the man himself.* And the Lord in the Gospel speaks in the hour of His Passion:[2] *Thou wouldest have no power against Me except it had been given thee from above.*

Now when we entreat that we may not come into temptation, we are warned by these words of our own infirmity and weakness, lest any one should insolently exalt himself, proudly and arrogantly assuming aught to himself, counting the glory of confession or of suffering as his own; whereas the Lord Himself taught humility in the injunction,[3] *Watch and pray, lest ye come into temptation. The spirit indeed is willing, but the flesh is weak.* Thus a humble and submissive confession comes first, and everything is referred to God, so that whatever we as suppliants ask in the fear and reverence of God may be supplied by His Fatherly kindness.

[1] Job i. 12.   [2] John xix. 11.
[3] Matt. xxvi. 41.

CHAPTER XXVII

AFTER all these petitions there comes at the end of the Prayer a short clause which in condensed brevity comprises the sum total of our requests and prayers. For we place at the very end these words: BUT DELIVER US FROM THE EVIL ONE, including everything that the enemy contrives against us in this world; a sure and safe security from which may be had if God deliver us and afford His aid when we entreat and implore.

Now having said DELIVER US FROM THE EVIL ONE, nothing remains beyond this for which we ought to make request, when once we have asked for God's protection against the evil one. For when that is granted we stand secure and safe against all that the devil and the world can do. For what fear can he have of the world who has God for his protector in the world?

CHAPTER XXVIII

WHAT wonder, dearly beloved brethren, if such is the Prayer which God taught, seeing that He condensed in His instruction all our petitioning in one saving phrase. This had already been foretold by the Prophet Isaiah when, full of the Holy

Spirit, he spake of the majesty and Fatherly kindness of God: *Summing up and cutting short His word in righteousness, because a short word will the Lord make in all the earth.*[1] For when the Word of God, our Lord Jesus Christ, came unto all and gathered together the learned and unlearned alike, and published to every sex and age the precepts of salvation, He made a sublime abridgment of His precepts, so that the memory of His disciples might, without being over-tasked in the heavenly rule, remember with readiness whatever was necessary for a simple faith. Thus, when He taught what is life eternal, He embraced the mysterious doctrine of life within a splendid and divine brevity, saying:[2] *Now this is life eternal, that they may know Thee, the only and true God, and Jesus Christ Whom Thou hast sent.* Likewise when He gathered from the Law and the Prophets the first and greater commandments, He said:[3] *Hear, O Israel, the Lord Thy God is One God; and thou shalt love the Lord thy God with all thy heart and with all thy mind and with all thy strength. This is the first commandment; and the second is like unto it: Thou shalt love thy neighbour*

---

[1] Isaiah x. 22. The old Latin version followed the LXX. translators in their misunderstanding of the Hebrew. Contrast St. Paul's use of the text in Rom. ix. 21.
[2] John xvii. 3.
[3] Mark xii. 29 (Deut. vi. 4); Matt. xxii. 40 (Levit. xix. 18).

as thyself. On these two commandments hang the whole Law and the Prophets. And again:[1] *Whatsoever good ye would that men should do unto you, do ye also unto them; for this is the Law and the Prophets.*

CHAPTER XXIX

NOR was it in words only, but also by His actions that the Lord taught us to pray, Himself praying often and beseeching, and thus shewing what we ought to do by the testimony of His own example; as it is written:[2] *He Himself departed into a solitary place and prayed.* And again,[3] *He went away into the mountain to pray, and continued all night in prayer to God.* But if He, Who was without sin, used to pray, how much more ought sinners to pray! And if He, keeping continual watch throughout the whole night, was offering unceasing prayer, how much more ought we to watch by night in oft-repeated prayer!

CHAPTER XXX

NOW the Lord was praying and beseeching not for Himself,—for what should He, innocent as He

[1] Matt. vii. 12.   [2] Luke v. 16.   [3] Luke vi. 12.

was, ask for Himself?—but for our sins; as He makes clear when He says to Peter: [1] *Lo, Satan was earnestly asking that he might sift you as wheat. But I have prayed for thee that thy faith fail not.* And, later on, He entreats for all, saying: [2] *I do not pray for these alone, but also for those who shall believe on Me through their word, that all may be one, as Thou, Father, art in Me and I in Thee, that they also may be in us.* Great is the lovingkindness of God and equally great His Fatherly pity regarding our salvation, Who, not content to redeem us with His Blood, also thus prayed so fully for us as well. See now what was the desire of His prayer—namely, that like as the Father and the Son are One, so also we may abide in very oneness. Hence may be understood how greatly he sins who rends unity and peace, because the Lord actually prayed for this unity, desiring that His people should have life, inasmuch as He knew that discord enters not into the kingdom of God.

CHAPTER XXXI

Now when we stand at prayer, dearly beloved brethren, it behoves us to be watchful and to enter

[1] Luke xxii. 31.   [2] John xvii. 20.

into our prayers with our whole heart. Let every carnal and worldly thought be put away, nor let the mind dwell upon anything else than the prayer it is offering. Hence it is that the priest before prayer utters a prefatory injunction and prepares the minds of the brethren by saying

Lift up your hearts,

in order that, while the people respond

We lift them up unto the Lord,

they may be warned that they ought to think of nothing but the Lord. Let the breast be closed against the adversary and open to *the only God*, nor let it suffer God's enemy to approach it in the time of prayer. For he creeps in oft and insinuates himself, and by subtil deceit calls away our prayers from God, so that we have one thing in our heart and another on our lips; whereas it is not the sound of the voice, but the mind and heart that ought to pray to the Lord with sincerity of intention.

What sluggishness is it to be led astray and captivated by unbecoming and profane thoughts when you supplicate the Lord, as if there were aught else that it behoved you to think of save that you are speaking with God! How can you ask to be heard of God when you do not even hear yourself? Do you expect the Lord to be mindful of you in your entreaties when you are not even mindful of yourself? This is to be entirely off your guard against the enemy: this is to offend the majesty of God by negligence in the prayers which you offer: this is to be awake with the eyes and to be asleep with the heart; whereas the Christian ought even when asleep with the eyes, to be awake with the heart, as it is written in the character of the Church speaking, in the Song of Songs:[1] *I sleep, and my heart waketh.* Wherefore the Apostle warns us solicitously and anxiously, saying,[2] *Continue in prayer, and watch in the same;* teaching, that is, and shewing that those are able to obtain what they ask from God whom He sees to be watchful in prayer.

CHAPTER XXXII

LET not, moreover, those who pray come to God with unfruitful or barren prayers. Prayer is ineffectual when the petition offered to God is sterile; for as *every tree which does not bear fruit is cut down and cast into the fire*,[3] most certainly also the utterance that has no fruit cannot be well-pleasing to God, because it is not abounding in any works. Hence Divine Scripture instructs us, saying:[4] *Prayer*

[1] Cant. v. 2.   [2] Col. iv. 2.
[3] Matt. vii. 19.   [4] Tobit xii. 8.

is good with fasting and alms. For He Who in the day of judgment will render a reward for works and alms is now also a gracious Hearer of one who comes to Him in prayer associated with works. Thus, for instance, Cornelius the centurion, when he prayed, deserved to be heard. For he was in the habit of doing many almsdeeds towards the people, and of constantly praying to God. And when he was praying about the ninth hour an angel stood by him, testifying to his works, and saying,[1] *Cornelius, thy prayers and thine alms have ascended for a memorial before God.*

CHAPTER XXXIII

QUICKLY do those prayers ascend to God which the merits of our works urge upon Him. And thus the angel Raphael assisted Tobias in his unceasing prayer and works, saying:[2] *It is honourable to reveal and make known the works of God. For when thou wast praying, thou and Sarah, I brought the memorial of your prayer before the holiness of God; and when thou didst bury the dead as a simple duty, and because thou didst not delay to rise up and leave thy breakfast, but didst depart to cover the dead, I also was sent to prove thee; and now*

[1] Acts x, 2, 4. [2] Tobit xii, 11.

again God hath sent me to heal thee and Sarah thy daughter-in-law. For I am Raphael, one of the seven righteous angels who stand by and wait before the holiness of God.

Through Isaiah also the Lord admonishes and teaches us likewise, attesting:[1] *Loosen every knot of unrighteousness: cancel the oppressions of invalid contracts. Send away the enfeebled in peace, and annul every unjust agreement. Break thy bread for the hungry, and bring in the homeless poor to thine house. When thou seest the naked clothe him, and despise not the household of thine own seed. Then shall thy light break forth in season, and thy raiment shall spring forth speedily, and justice shall go before thee, and the glory of the Lord shall surround thee. Then shalt thou call and God will hear thee: as soon as thou speakest, He saith, Lo, here am I.* He promises to be present, and says that He hears and protects those who loosen the knots of unrighteousness from their heart, and do alms-deeds to God's household according to His precepts. Because they hear what God commands to be done, they themselves deserve to be heard by God.

The blessed Apostle Paul, when aided by the brethren in stress of persecution, said that the works which they did were sacrifices to God. *I am filled,* saith he,[2] *having received from Epaphro-*

---

[1] Isaiah lviii. 6.   [2] Phil. iv. 18.

ditus the things which were sent by you, an odour of a sweet smell, a sacrifice acceptable and pleasing to God. For since *he that hath pity upon the poor hath lent to God*,[1] and he who *gives to the little ones*[2] gives to God, he doth sacrifice spiritually to God *an odour of a sweet smell.*

CHAPTER XXXIV

Now in the offering of prayer we find that the Three Children with Daniel, being strong in faith and victors even in captivity, observed the third, sixth, and ninth hours,[3] in as it were a symbol of the Trinity Which in these last times should be revealed. For the progress of the first hour to the third shows the perfected number of the Trinity; likewise from the fourth to the sixth declares another Trinity; and when the period from the seventh to the ninth is completed, the perfect Trinity is numbered through a triad of hours each.

These spaces of hours were long ago fixed upon by the worshippers of God, who observed them as the appointed and lawful times for prayer. After-events have made it manifest that of old these

[1] Prov. xix. 17. [2] Matt. x. 42.
[3] Compare Dan. vi. 10.

THE LORD'S PRAYER 67

were types, inasmuch as righteous men thus formerly prayed. For at the third hour the Holy Spirit descended upon the disciples and fulfilled the gracious promise of the Lord. Likewise at the sixth hour Peter, going up to the house-top, was instructed as well by the sign as by the voice of God bidding him admit all to the grace of salvation, when he was doubtful previously whether Gentiles ought to be cleansed. And from the sixth to the ninth hour the Lord, being crucified, washed away our sins in His own Blood; and that He might redeem and quicken us He then perfected His victory by His Passion.

CHAPTER XXXV

BUT for us, dearly beloved brethren, in addition to the hours anciently observed, both the times and the rules of prayer have now increased in number. For we must pray also in the morning, in order that the Resurrection of the Lord may be celebrated by morning prayer. And this the Holy Spirit formerly pointed out in the Psalms, saying,[1] *My King and my God! for unto Thee will I pray, O Lord, in the morning, and Thou shalt hear my voice: in the morning will I stand to Thee, and I*

[1] Psal. v. 3.

shall see Thee. And again, the Lord speaks by the Prophet:[1] *Early in the morning shall they watch for Me, saying, Let us go and return unto the Lord our God.* Likewise at sunset and the decline of day must we needs pray again. For since Christ is the true Sun and true Day, when we pray at the decline of the world's sun and day and entreat that the light may again come upon us, we are asking for the Advent of Christ, which will bestow on us the grace of eternal light. The Holy Spirit declares in the Psalms that Christ is called the Day. *The stone,* He says,[2] *which the builders refused is become the head of the corner. This has been done by the Lord, and it is marvellous in our eyes. This is the Day which the Lord hath made: let us rejoice and feast in it.* Also that He is called the Sun, the Prophet Malachi testifies, saying:[3] *But unto you that fear the Name of the Lord shall the Sun of Righteousness arise, and in His wings is Healing.* But if in the Holy Scriptures Christ is the true Sun and true Day, there is no hour excepted when Christians ought not constantly and continually to worship God; so that we who are in Christ—that is, in the true Sun and Day—may all day long be instant in entreaties and prayers; and when by the world's law the revolving night, recurring in its

[1] Hos. vi. 1.   [2] Psal. cxviii. 22.
[3] Mal. iv. 2.

alternate changes, succeeds, there can be no loss to us from its nocturnal shades, because to the sons of light it is day even in the night. For when can he be without light who has the Light in his heart? Or when is the sun and the day not his to whom Christ is both Sun and Day?

CHAPTER XXXVI

LET us then, who are ever in Christ—that is, in the Light—cease not from prayer even by night. Thus the widow Anna without ceasing persevered with constant prayer and watching in being well-pleasing to God ; as it is written in the Gospel :[1] *She departed not from the temple, serving with fastings and prayers night and day.*

It is no relief to us that there are Gentiles who have not yet been enlightened, or Jews who have deserted the light and abide in darkness. Let us, dearly beloved brethren, who are ever in the light of the Lord, and who remember and hold fast what we have begun to be by grace given, reckon for "day." Let us deem ourselves to be ever walking in the light ; let us not be hindered by the darkness from which we have escaped ; let there be no loss of prayers in the night hours, no idle and

[1] Luke ii. 37.

slothful time-losing in opportunities of prayer. Let us, spiritually recreated and born again by the tender mercy of God, imitate that which we are destined to be; for since in the Kingdom we shall have day only without intervention of night, let us so watch by night as if in the light; and since we are to pray and give thanks to God for ever, let us not cease here also to offer prayers and thanksgivings.

APPENDIX

Containing some passages from the Treatise of Tertullian
"On Prayer" (De Oratione).

In view of the fact that St. Cyprian's work was partly modelled on Tertullian's, it seemed well to add in this Appendix some of the most striking of Tertullian's passages in illustration of St. Cyprian's treatise.

The translation is a free one, based upon that in the Oxford "Library of the Fathers," vol. i.

I

JESUS CHRIST, Spirit and Word and Reason of God, gave to the disciples of the New Covenant a new form of Prayer. It was needed as new wine in new skins. . . . The old things having been either changed (as circumcision), or fulfilled (as the Law), or accomplished (as prophecy), or perfected (as faith), the new grace of God fashioned anew all things and brought in the Gospel as the expunger of the past. . . . John also taught his disciples to pray, but John's work was to prepare the way for Christ—himself to decrease and Christ to increase; and so the forerunner's work passed to the Lord. Hence John's form of Prayer has not been preserved, because the earthly has given way to the heavenly. Let us note three things: first, Christ's heavenly wisdom in the command to pray in secret, believing that the eye and the ear of Almighty God are present under coverings and in secret places; secondly, His requiring a modesty of faith whereby religious service is offered to Him alone Who heareth and seeth everywhere; thirdly, His forbidding us to think that God must be approached with a multitude of words. This brevity of the Prayer does but accentuate the breadth of interpretation possible to its words. The Prayer is indeed as much expanded in meaning as it is condensed in expression. It embraces not only the proper functions of prayer—worship of God, and petitioning of man—but almost every teaching of the Lord, every reminder of the Christian rule of life, so that it comprises a breviary of the whole Gospel.

II

THE Prayer begins with a testimony to God and a reward of faith, for we say, OUR FATHER WHO ART IN HEAVEN. Herein we both pray to God and commend the faith whose reward it is thus to entitle Him. It is written: *To them that believed on Him gave He power to be called the sons of God.*

Although indeed the Lord hath very frequently proclaimed God to us as a Father, and hath moreover taught us to call no man Father upon earth, save only Him Whom we have in heaven. So that in thus praying we obey a commandment.

But in calling Him FATHER we also recognize Him as God. "FATHER" implies affectionate care as well as authority. Besides, in the Father the Son also is invoked; for He saith, *I and the Father are One.* Nor is even the Mother Church omitted; if indeed in the Father and the Son the Mother also be recognized, from whom the Name of Father and Son comes into being.[1]

III

THE Name of God the Father had been disclosed to no one. . . . To us it has been revealed in the Son. For "Son" is now a new Name of the Father. *I am come,* He says, *in My Father's Name.* We ask therefore that this NAME may BE HALLOWED. . . . We pray that it may be hallowed in us who are in Him, and at the same time in all others whom the grace of God yet awaiteth. Herein we obey a commandment in praying for all, even for our enemies.

[1] The thought is obscurely expressed. Tertullian appears to mean that the Name of Father on its divine side implies the Son, and on its earthly side implies a mother, the Church. So St. Cyprian does not hesitate to say, "He cannot have God as his Father who has not the Church as his Mother" (*De eccl. unit.* 6).

IV

WE add, THY WILL BE DONE IN HEAVEN AND IN EARTH. Not that any one can hinder the doing of God's will, but we ask that His will may be done in all men. For by a figurative interpretation of flesh and spirit we are heaven and earth. Although even if it is to be understood simply, the sense of the petition is the same; namely, that in us the will of God may be done in earth, so that it may be done in heaven also. Now what doth God will, save that we should walk according to His rule? We ask Him therefore to supply us with the substance and power of His will that we may be saved both in heaven and in earth, seeing that the sum of His will is the salvation of those whom He has adopted. That also is the will of God which the Lord performed in preaching, in working, and in enduring. For so did He Himself declare, that He did not His own will but the will of the Father. . . .

Likewise when we say THY WILL BE DONE, we wish well to ourselves, because there is naught of evil in the will of God, even if according to the deserts of each somewhat contrariwise be inflicted. In so saying then we exhort ourselves unto patience. . . . .

V

THY KINGDOM COME has the same reference as THY WILL BE DONE, namely, in ourselves.

For when does God not reign, in Whose hand is the heart of all things? But whatever we wish for ourselves, we divine to be His, and we attribute to Him what we await from Him. It is inconsistent to pray, as some do, for the prolongation of the world, when the Coming of the Kingdom means the consummation of the world. We desire to reign the sooner, not to serve the longer. . . . The avenging of the martyrs, too, is regulated by the end of the world. . . . Speedily let THY KINGDOM COME, O Lord! the Christian's prayer, the nations' confusion, the Angel's joy, for which we are persecuted,—for which we the rather pray!

VI

How beautifully hath Divine Wisdom arranged the order of the Prayer, so that after celestial things—the Name of God, the Will of God, and the Kingdom of God—a place should now be given to earthly wants. This is as the Lord had commanded, *Seek ye first the Kingdom and then these things shall be added unto you.*

Yet we may rather understand spiritually, GIVE US THIS DAY OUR DAILY BREAD. For Christ is our Bread, because Christ is Life and bread is life. *I am the Bread of Life,* He said; and just before, *The Bread is the Word of the Living God which cometh down from heaven.* Then again, because His Body is understood to be in the Bread, He said, *This is My Body.*

Wherefore in praying for DAILY BREAD, we pray to be perpetually in Christ and inseparable from His Body.

Yet because the word has also a physical meaning, we have this command to pray for bread only as a religious rule. Bread alone is necessary for the faithful ; *the rest the Gentiles seek after.*

GIVE US THIS DAY is inserted because He had previously taught, *Take no thought for the morrow what ye shall eat;* and illustrated the point by the parable of the rich fool.

VII

HAVING observed the bounty of God we now pray for His mercy. . . . The Lord knew that He alone was without sin. He therefore teaches us to pray, FORGIVE US OUR DEBTS. Prayer for forgiveness is a confession of sin . . . and thus repentance is shewn, acceptable to God, because He willeth this rather than the death of a sinner. Now in Scripture a debt is a metaphor for a sin. The parable of the unforgiving servant illustrates this, and with this agrees our profession that we FORGIVE OUR DEBTORS. Moreover, in another place He saith on this aspect of the Prayer, *Forgive, and it shall be forgiven you.*

VIII

FOR the completing of this wondrously compendious Prayer, in order that we should pray

APPENDIX 77

not only for forgiveness, but for the entire turning away of sins, He added, LEAD US NOT INTO TEMPTATION : that is, Suffer us not to be led —of course, by him that tempteth. Far be it that the Lord should be thought to tempt. . . . When He was tempted of the devil He shewed who was the head and contriver of temptation. . . . And thus the clause corresponds—BUT DELIVER US FROM THE EVIL ONE.

IX

IN this brief epitome how many sayings of the Prophets, Gospels, Apostles, discourses of the Lord, examples, precepts are touched upon! How many duties at once discharged! The honouring of God in the Father, the testimony of faith in the Name, the offering of obedience in the will, the remembrance of hope in the kingdom, the petition for life in the bread, the confession of debts in the deprecation, the solicitude concerning temptations in the demand for defence. What wonder? God alone could teach how He wished to be prayed to. This Prayer then, offered as a duty, ordained by Himself and animated by His own spirit, since it emanated from the Divine lips, ascends by its own right into heaven, commending to the Father what the Son taught.

X

YET the Lord, foreseeing human needs, after delivering the rule of Prayer, added, *Ask and ye shall receive*, meaning that it is allowable to add upon the foundation additional desires, yet alway mindful of the Commandments.

XI

THE remembrance of the Commandments paves the way for prayers to heaven; the chief of which is, that we approach not the altar of God before we have reconciled all quarrels or enmity with our brethren. For what kind of action is it to approach unto *the peace of God* without peace? unto the remission of debts while retaining them?

. . . .

XVII

WE shall commend our prayers before God, if we pray with modesty and humility, not even our hands being lifted up too high, but with moderation and seemliness, nor our face being raised with boldness. For the Tax-gatherer who prayed humbled and abased, not only in his prayer but in his countenance, went away justified rather than the impudent Pharisee. We should also subdue the tone of our voice; for it is not of the voice but of the heart that God is the hearer and the seer likewise. . . . What more shall they gain who pray more loudly than others, save that they stun their neighbours?

. . . .

[*Tertullian concludes with one of the noblest of perorations.*]

XXVIII

WE are the true worshippers and the true priests, who, praying in spirit, would offer up in spirit the Prayer of God, His own and acceptable, as that which He hath required and provided. This, dedicated from the whole heart, nourished by faith, adorned by truth, whole in innocence, pure in chastity, crowned by love, we ought to lead up to the altar of God, with a procession of good works amid psalms and hymns, as destined to obtain all things for us from God.

For what hath God Who requireth it denied to the prayer that cometh of spirit and of truth? We read and hear and believe how great are the proofs of its efficacy. Of old prayer used to deliver from fires and beasts and famine, and yet it had not then received its form from Christ. How much more copiously, then, will Christian prayer prevail! It furnishes with patience those who suffer and feel and grieve, it supplements grace with valour. It is prayer alone that conquers God. Consequently it avails to recall the souls of the departed from the pathway of death, to recover the weak, to heal the sick, to exorcize the dæmoniacs, to open the gates of the prison, to loose the bonds of the innocent. This it is that washes away sins, repels temptations, quenches persecutions, consoles the weak-hearted, delights the great-hearted, brings back travellers, stills the waves, stupifies brigands, nourishes the poor, rules the rich, directs the sick, raises the lapsed, upholds the falling, sustains the standing.

Prayer is the wall of faith, our armour and our weapons against the enemy who watches us on every side. Therefore let us never walk unarmed. By day let us be mindful of our station, by night of our vigil. Under the arms of prayer let us guard the standard of our Captain, in prayer let us await the trumpet of the angel. Even the angels all pray. Every creature prayeth. The cattle and wild beasts pray and bend their knees, and as they go forth from their stalls and caves look up to heaven, not with silent mouth, making their breath vibrate after their own manner. Even the birds as they soar from their nest strain towards heaven, stretching out the cross of their wings for hands, and utter what may well be a prayer.

What more, then, of the duty of prayer? The Lord Himself prayed—to Whom be honour and power for ever and ever.

INDEX

I.—SCRIPTURAL.

	PAGE		PAGE
Lev. xix. 18	. 59	Matthew vi. 6	. 28
Deut. vi. 4	. 59	,, 9 f.	. 5, 19, 32
,, xxxiii. 9	. 35	,, 31	. 50
1 Sam. i. 13	. 30	,, 34	. 48
,, ii. 30	. 38	,, vii. 2	. 53
1 Kings xi. 14	. 56	,, 12	. 60
2 Kings xxiv. 11	. 56	,, 19	. 63
Job i. 12	. 57	,, viii. 11	. 41
Psalm iv. 4	. 30	,, 22	. 35
,, v. 3	. 67	,, x. 42	. 66
,, xxxvii. 25	. 50	,, xviii. 32	. 52
,, lxviii. 6	. 34	,, 34	. 53
,, cxviii. 22	. 68	,, xix. 21	. 50
Prov. x. 3	. 50	,, xxii. 40	. 59
,, xv. 3	. 29	,, xxiii. 8	. 35
,, xix. 17	. 66	,, xxv. 34	. 40
Cant. v. 2	. 63	,, xxvi. 39	. 42
Isaiah i. 3 f.	. 36	,, 41	. 57
,, x. 22	. 59	Mark vii. 8	. 27
,, xlii. 25	. 56	,, xi. 25	. 21, 53
,, lviii. 6	. 65	,, xii. 29	. 59
Jerem. xxiii. 23 f.	. 28	Luke i. 79	. 25
Dan. iii. 51	. 33	,, ii. 37	. 69
,, vi. 10	. 66	,, v. 16	. 60
Hosea vi 1	. 68	,, 22	. 29
Mal. iv. 2	. 68	,, vi. 12	. 60
Tobit xii. 8	. 63	,, xi. 1 ff.	. 6, 19
,, 11	. 64	,, xii. 20	. 49
Baruch vi 6	. 30	,, xiv. 33	. 48
Matthew v. 13	. 45	,, xviii. 10	. 21, 31
,, 24	. 54	,, xx. 7	. 38
,, 44	. 45	,, xxi. 31	. 61
,, 45	. 46	John i. 11	. 34

INDEX

		PAGE		PAGE
John	iii. 5	. 46	1 Cor. vi. 9 .	. 39
,,	iv. 23	. 26	,, 20 .	. 38
,,	v. 14	. 39	,, x. 13 .	. 19
,,	vi. 38	. 42	,, xv. 47 .	. 45
,,	48	. 46	Gal. v. 17 .	. 44
,,	51	. 47	Ephes. iv. 4 .	. 54
,,	53	. 47	Philip. iv. 18	. 65
,,	viii. 34	. 37	Coloss. iv. 2 .	. 63
,,	44	. 36	1 Tim. vi. 7 .	. 49
,,	xiv. 6	. 27	,, 9 .	. 19
,,	xvi. 23	. 28	1 Pet. i. 16 .	. 38
,,	xvii. 3	. 59	1 John i. 8	. 52
,,	20	. 61	,, ii. 1	. 27
,,	xix. 11	. 57	,, 15	. 42
Acts i. 14		. 34	,, iii. 15	. 55
,, x. 2 f.		. 64	Rev. ii. 23	. 29
Rom. ix. 21		. 59	,, vi. 10	. 55

II.—General.

Abel 54	Curubis 12
Adrumetum 6	Cyprian, St., Life . . .7 f.
Ægypt 11	,, in English Kalendar . 13
Æthiopia 11	,, on Lord's Prayer 5, 14
"African" text . . . 16	,, on Unity of the Church 14
Alexander 10	Cyril's Catecheses . . . 21
Ambrose, St. . . . 5	
Anna 29	Decius, Edict of . . 9, 14
Augustine, St. 6, 8, 16 f., 23, 39	De Oratione Dom., Date of . 14
	Dionysius of Alexandria . 19
Babylas 10	Donatus 8
Benson, Archbp. . . 6, 13	Dowden, Bp. . . . 21
Bright, Dr. W. . . . 22	Duchesne 20
Caecilianus 8	
Caesarians 12	Eucharist, The Holy . 20, 22
Cain 54	,, received daily . 47
Chase, Dr. . . . 15, 19	
Church, The, our Mother . 73	Fabian 10
Clement of Alexandria . 22 f.	
Cornelius, centurion . . 64	Galerius Maximus . . 13
Cornelius of Rome . . 11	Goths 10
Councils at Karthage . 11 f.	Greece 11
Crashaw, R., quoted . . 31	Gregory Nyssen . . . 20

INDEX

	PAGE		PAGE
Hilary, St.	5	Plague, The Great	11
Hippo	23	Pontius, deacon	9
Hippolytus, Canons of	20	Prayer, Standing at	21
		,, Hours of	23, 66 f.
Jerome, St., quoted	8	,, John's form of	72
Job	57	Priscus	10
John the Baptist	71 f.		
		Raphael, the Angel	64
Karthage	10		
		Satan	56
Lactantius	8	"Station Days"	23
Léonard, l'Abbé	7	*Sursum Corda*	20 f., 62
Liturgies, Early	19	Syria	11
Macrianus	12	Tertullian	5, 16, 20, 22
Martyrdom	55	Three Holy Children	33, 66
Mozarabic missal	21	Tobias	64
		Trinity, Symbolism of the Holy 66 f.	
Novatianists	11		
		Valerian, Edict of	12
Paternoster, Text of	15	Vincent, St.	5
,, Efficacy of	39		
Pelagianism	6	Watson, E. W.	6
Pharisee and tax-gatherer	30 f.	Wordsworth, quoted	27

PUBLICATIONS

OF THE

SOCIETY FOR PROMOTING CHRISTIAN KNOWLEDGE.

EARLY CHURCH CLASSICS.
Small post 8vo, cloth boards, 1s. each.

A Homily of Clement of Alexandria, entitled, Who is the Rich Man that is Being Saved? By Rev. P. MORDAUNT BARNARD.

Bishop Sarapion's Prayer-Book: An Egyptian Pontifical dated probably about 350–356 A.D. Translated from the Edition of Dr. G. WOBBERMIN. With Introduction, Notes, and Indices, by the Right Rev. JOHN WORDSWORTH, D.D. 1s. 6d.

St. Polycarp, Bishop of Smyrna. By the Rev. BLOMFIELD JACKSON, M.A.

The Doctrine of the Twelve Apostles. Translated into English, with Introduction and Notes, by the Rev. CHARLES BIGG, D.D.

The Epistle of St. Clement, Bishop of Rome. By the Rev. JOHN A. F. GREGG, M.A.

St. Augustine's Treatise on the City of God. By Rev. F. R. M. HITCHCOCK, M.A., B.D. 1s. 6d.

The Epistle of the Gallican Churches: Lugdunum and Vienna. With an Appendix containing Tertullian's Address to Martyrs and the Passion of St. Perpetua. Translated, with Introduction and Notes, by Rev. T. HERBERT BINDLEY, B.D.

The Epistles of St. Ignatius, Bishop of Antioch. By Rev. J. H. SRAWLEY, M.A. In two volumes. 1s. each.

The Liturgy of the Eighth Book of "the Apostolic Constitutions," commonly called the Clementine Liturgy. Translated into English, with Introduction and Notes, by Rev. R. H. CRESSWELL, M.A. 1s. 6d.

The Shepherd of Hermas. By the Rev. C. TAYLOR, D.D., Master of St. John's College, Cambridge. Vol. I. 2s.

THE
DAWN OF EUROPEAN LITERATURE.

A set of Works designed to present the chief races of Europe as they emerge out of pre-historic darkness into the light furnished by their earliest recorded words.

Post 8vo, cloth boards, 2s. 6d. each.

Anglo-Saxon Literature. By the Rev. Professor EARLE.
French Literature. By the late GUSTAVE MASSON, B.A.
Slavonic Literature. By W. R. MORFILL, M.A.
The Greek Epic. By GEORGE C. W. WARR, M.A. 3s.

THE
FATHERS FOR ENGLISH READERS.

A Series of Monographs on the Chief Fathers of the Church, the Fathers selected being centres of influence at important periods of Church History, and in important spheres of action.

Fcap. 8vo, cloth boards, 2s. each.

Boniface. By the Rev. Canon GREGORY SMITH. 1s. 6d.
Clement of Alexandria. By the Rev. F. R. MONTGOMERY HITCHCOCK, B.D. 3s.
Leo the Great. By the Right Rev. C. GORE, D.D.
Gregory the Great. By the late Rev. J. BARMBY, B.D.
Saint Ambrose: his Life, Times, and Teaching. By the Venerable Archdeacon THORNTON, D.D.
Saint Athanasius: his Life and Times. By the Rev. R. WHELER BUSH. 2s. 6d.
Saint Augustine. By the Rev. E. L. CUTTS, D.D.
Saint Basil the Great. By the Rev. R. T. SMITH, B.D.
Saint Bernard: Abbot of Clairvaux, A.D. 1091-1153. By Rev. S. J. EALES. 2s. 6d.
Saint Jerome. By the Rev. EDWARD L. CUTTS, D.D.
Saint Hilary of Poitiers, and Saint Martin of Tours. By the Rev. J. GIBSON CAZENOVE, D.D.
Saint John of Damascus. By the Rev. J. H. LUPTON.
Saint Patrick: his Life and Teaching. By the Rev. E. J. NEWELL, M.A. 2s. 6d.
Synesius of Cyrene, Philosopher and Bishop. By ALICE GARDNER.
The Apostolic Fathers. By the Rev. Canon SCOTT HOLLAND.
The Defenders of the Faith; or, The Christian Apologists of the Second and Third Centuries. By the Rev. F. WATSON, D.D.
The Venerable Bede. By the Right Rev. G. F. BROWNE.

CHIEF ANCIENT PHILOSOPHIES.

This Series deals with the chief systems of Ancient Thought, not merely as dry matters of History, but as having a bearing on Modern Speculation.

Fcap. 8vo, cloth boards, 2s. 6d. each.

Neoplatonism. By the Rev. C. BIGG, D.D. 3s.
Platonism. By the Rev. THOMAS B. STRONG, M.A. 3s.
Epicureanism. By the late Professor WILLIAM WALLACE.
Stoicism. By Rev. W. W. CAPES, Fellow of Hertford College.
Aristotelianism. The Ethics of Aristotle. By the Rev. I. GREGORY SMITH. The Logical Treatises, the Metaphysics, the Psychology, the Politics. By the Rev. W. GRUNDY.

DIOCESAN HISTORIES.

This Series furnishes a perfect Library of English Ecclesiastical History. Each volume is complete in itself, and the possibility of repetition has been carefully guarded against.

Fcap. 8vo, with Map, cloth boards.

Bath and Wells. By the Rev. W. HUNT. 2s. 6d.
Canterbury. By the late Rev. R. C. JENKINS. 3s. 6d.
Carlisle. By the late RICHARD S. FERGUSON. 2s. 6d.
Chester. By the Rev. RUPERT H. MORRIS. With Map. 3s.
Chichester. By the late Very Rev. W. R. W. STEPHENS. With Map and Plan. 2s. 6d.
Durham. By Rev. J. L. Low. With Map and Plan. 2s.
Hereford. By the late Rev. Canon PHILLPOTT. 3s.
Lichfield. By the Rev. W. BERESFORD. 2s. 6d.
Lincoln. By the late Rev. Canon E. VENABLES, and the late Ven. Archdeacon PERRY. With Map. 4s.
Llandaff. By the Rev. E. J. NEWELL, M.A. With Map. 3s. 6d.

Norwich. By the Rev. A. JESSOPP, D.D. 2s. 6d.
Oxford. By the Rev. E. MARSHALL. 2s. 6d.
Peterborough. By the Rev. G. A. POOLE, M.A. 2s. 6d.
Rochester. By the Rev. A. J. PEARMAN. With Map. 4s.
Salisbury. By the Rev. W. H. JONES. With Map. 2s. 6d.
Sodor and Man. By A. W. MOORE, M.A. 3s.
St. Asaph. By the Ven. Archdeacon THOMAS. 2s.
St. David's. By the Rev. Canon BEVAN. With Map. 2s. 6d.
Winchester. By the Rev. W. BENHAM, B.D. 3s.
Worcester. By the Rev. I. GREGORY SMITH and Rev. PHIPPS ONSLOW. 3s. 6d.
York. By the Rev. Canon ORNSBY, M.A., F.S.A. 3s. 6d.

NON-CHRISTIAN RELIGIOUS SYSTEMS.

Fcap. 8vo, cloth boards, 2s. 6d. each.

Buddhism: being a sketch of the Life and Teachings of Gautama, the Buddha. By T. W. RHYS DAVIDS, M.A., Ph.D. With Map.

Buddhism in China. By the Rev. S. BEAL. With Map.

Christianity and Buddhism: a Comparison and a Contrast. By the Rev. T. STERLING BERRY, D.D.

Confucianism and Taouism. By Professor ROBERT K. DOUGLAS, of the British Museum. With Map.

Hinduism. By the late Sir M. MONIER-WILLIAMS, M.A., D.C.L. With Map.

Islam and its Founder. By J. W. H. STOBART. With Map.

Islam as a Missionary Religion. By CHARLES R. HAINES. 2s.

The Coran: its Composition and Teaching, and the Testimony it bears to the Holy Scriptures. By Sir WILLIAM MUIR, K.C.S.I.

The Religion of the Crescent, or Islam: its Strength, its Weakness, its Origin, its Influence. By the Rev. W. ST. CLAIR TISDALL, M.A. 4s.

Studies of Non-Christian Religions. By ELIOT HOWARD.

COLONIAL CHURCH HISTORIES.

Fcap. 8vo, with Map, cloth boards.

Diocese of Mackenzie River, by the Right Rev. W. C. BOMPAS, D.D., Bishop of the Diocese. 2s.

New Zealand, by the late Very Rev. HENRY JACOBS, D.D., Dean of Christchurch. Containing the Dioceses of Auckland, Christchurch, Dunedin, Nelson, Waiapu, Wellington and Melanesia. 5s.

History of the Church in Eastern Canada and Newfoundland, by the Rev. J. LANGTRY. 3s.

The Church in the West Indies, by the Rev. A. CALDECOTT, B.D. 3s. 6d.

The Story of the Australian Church, by the Rev. E. SYMONDS. 2s. 6d.

LONDON: NORTHUMBERLAND AVENUE, W.C.